BUNNY SUICIDES

A POSTCARD BOOK

ANDY RILEY

A PLUME BOOK

Penguin Group (USA) Inc., 375 Hudson Street, New York, New York 10014, U.S.A.
Penguin Group (Canada), 90 Eglinton Avenue East, Suite 700, Toronto, Ontario, Canada M4P 2Y3 (a division of Pearson Penguin Canada Inc.)
Penguin Books Ltd., 80 Strand, London WC2R 0RL, England
Penguin Ireland, 25 St. Stephen's Green, Dublin 2, Ireland (a division of Penguin Books Ltd.)
Penguin Group (Australia), 250 Camberwell Road, Camberwell, Victoria 3124, Australia (a division of Pearson Australia Group Pty. Ltd.)
Penguin Books India Pvt. Ltd., 11 Community Centre, Panchsheel Park, New Delhi – 110 017, India
Penguin Books (NZ), Cnr Airborne and Rosedale Roads, Albany, Auckland 1310, New Zealand (a division of Pearson New Zealand Ltd.)
Penguin Books (South Africa) (Pty.) Ltd., 24 Sturdee Avenue, Rosebank, Johannesburg 2196, South Africa

First published by Plume, a member of Penguin Group (USA) Inc.

First Printing, October 2005

Cartoons first appeared in The Book of Bunny Suicides (Plume).

ISBN 0-452-28703-0

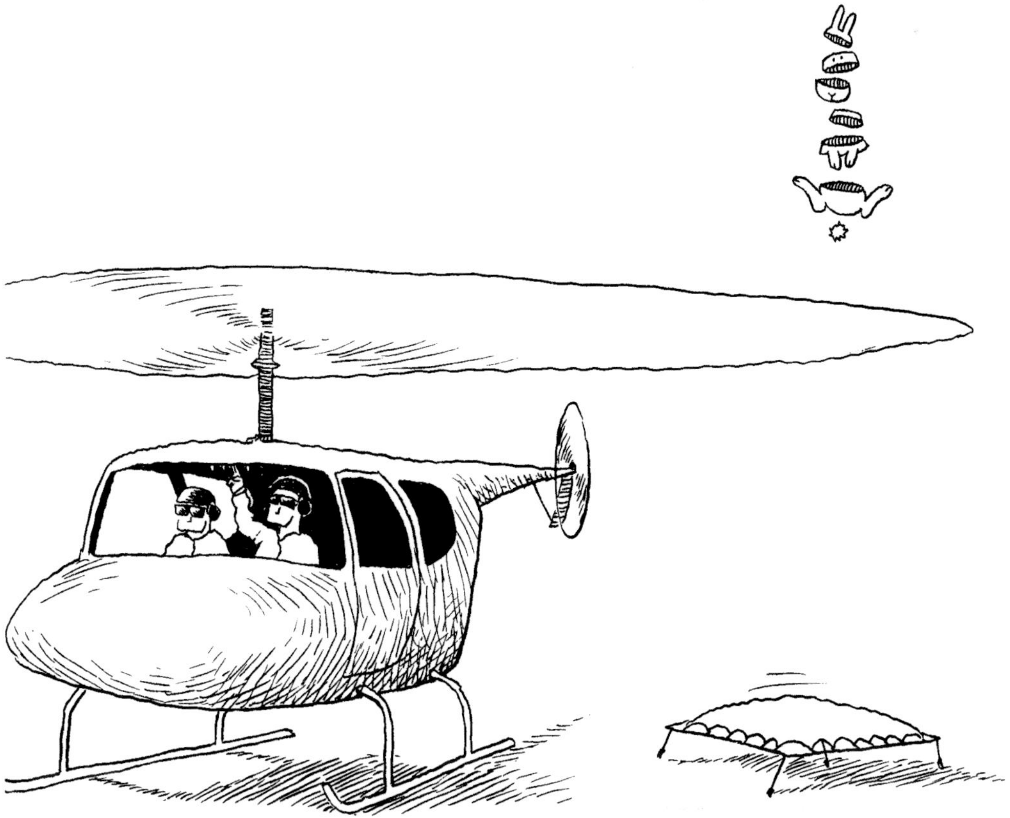

From: THE BOOK OF BUNNY SUICIDES

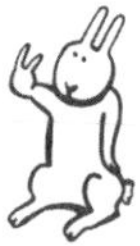

Little Fluffy Rabbits who Just Don't want to Live anymore

"It's the funniest, bunniest book I've ever read!"
—Elton John

"Brilliantly researched—one of the most important books of the year."
—Hugh Grant

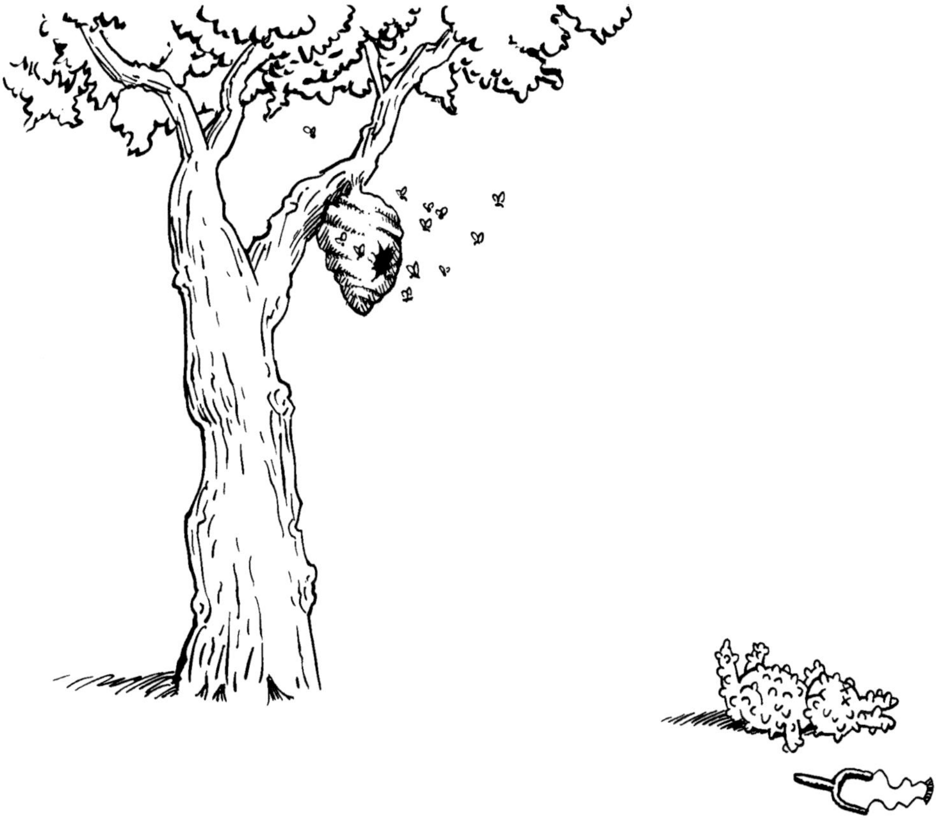

From: THE BOOK OF BUNNY SUICIDES

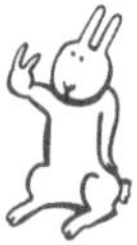

Little Fluffy Rabbits who Just Don't want to Live anymore

"It's the funniest, bunniest book I've ever read!"
—Elton John

"Brilliantly researched—one of the most important books of the year."
—Hugh Grant

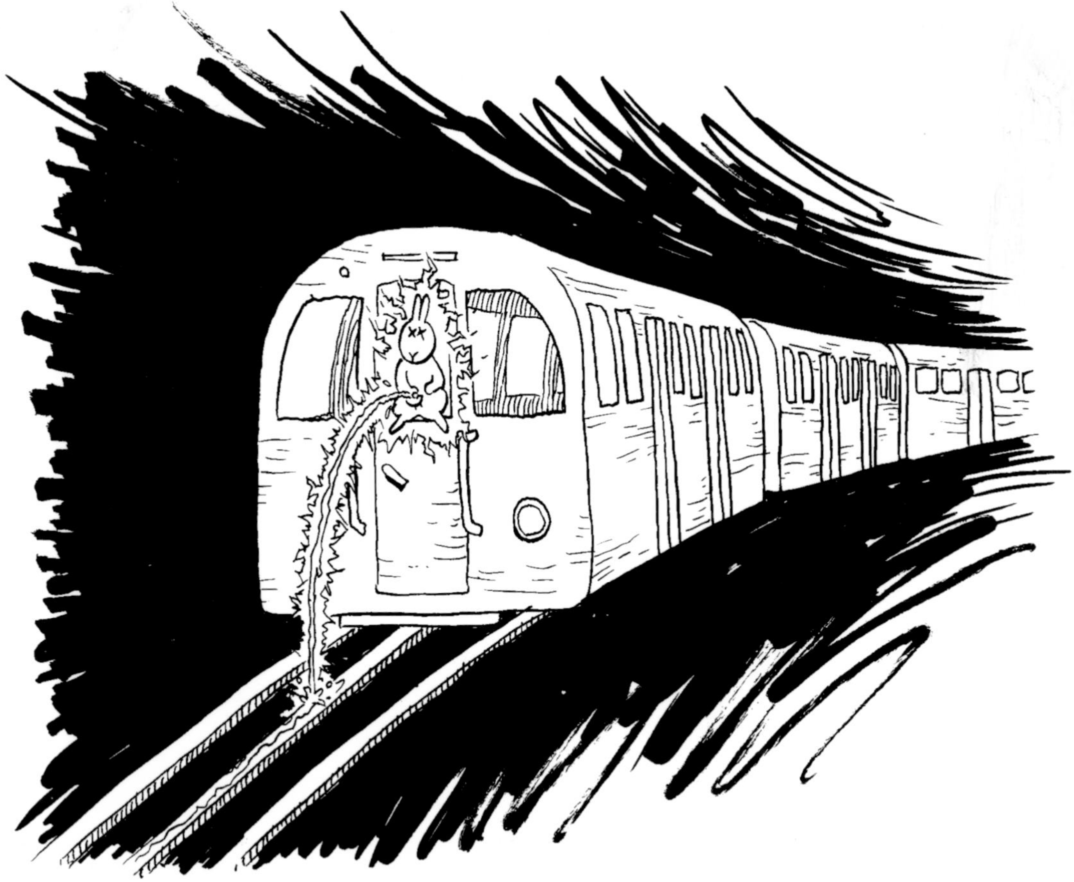

From: THE BOOK OF BUNNY SUICIDES

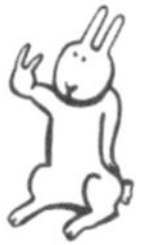

Little Fluffy Rabbits who Just Don't want to Live anymore

"It's the funniest, bunniest book I've ever read!"
—Elton John

"Brilliantly researched—one of the most important books of the year."
—Hugh Grant

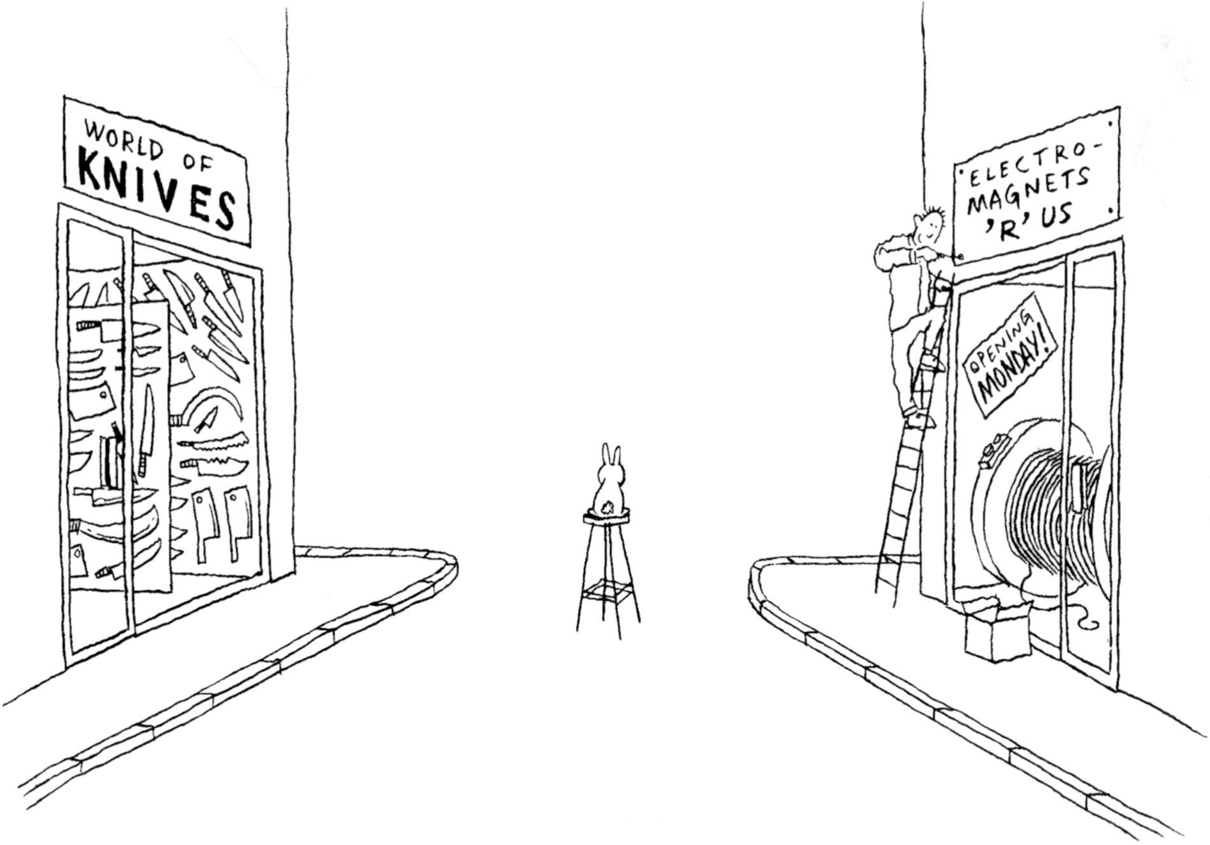
WORLD OF KNIVES
ELECTRO-MAGNETS 'R' US
OPENING MONDAY!

From: THE BOOK OF BUNNY SUICIDES

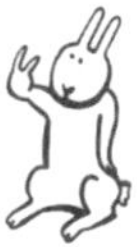

Little Fluffy Rabbits who Just Don't want to Live anymore

"It's the funniest, bunniest book I've ever read!"
—Elton John

"Brilliantly researched—one of the most important books of the year."
—Hugh Grant

From: THE BOOK OF BUNNY SUICIDES

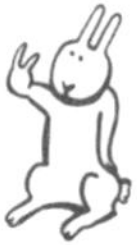

Little Fluffy Rabbits who Just Don't want to Live anymore

"It's the funniest, bunniest book I've ever read!"
—Elton John

"Brilliantly researched—one of the most important books of the year."
—Hugh Grant

From: THE BOOK OF BUNNY SUICIDES

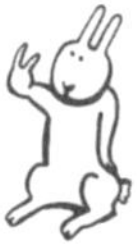

Little Fluffy Rabbits who Just Don't want to Live anymore

"It's the funniest, bunniest book I've ever read!"
—Elton John

"Brilliantly researched—one of the most important books of the year."
—Hugh Grant

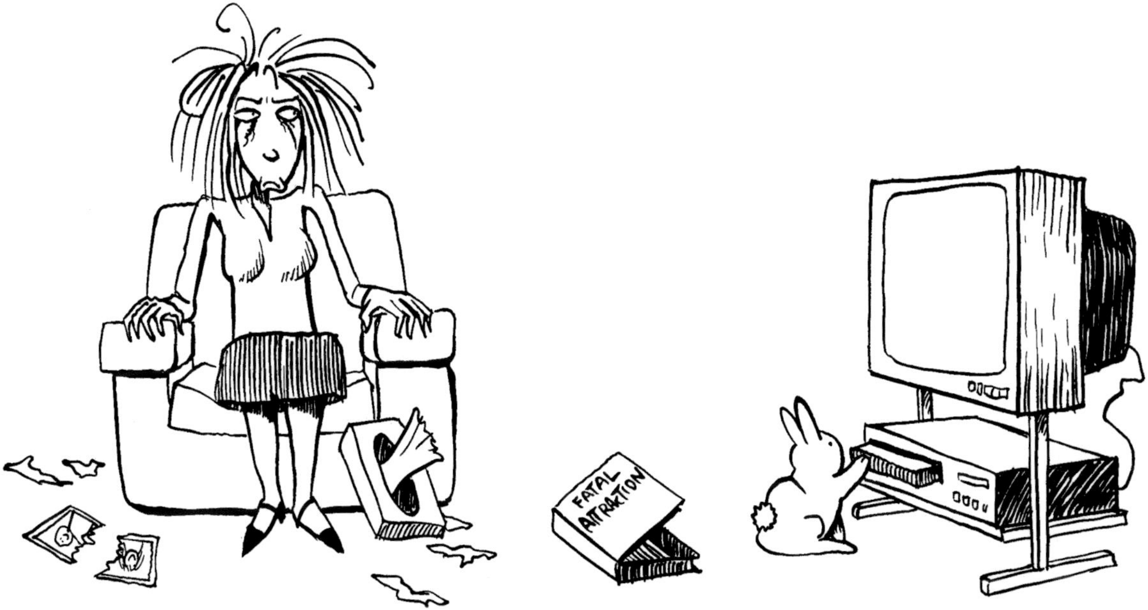
FATAL
ATTRAKTION

From: THE BOOK OF BUNNY SUICIDES

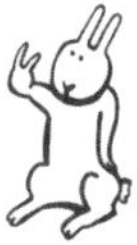

Little Fluffy Rabbits who Just Don't want to Live anymore

"It's the funniest, bunniest book I've ever read!"
—Elton John

"Brilliantly researched—one of the most important books of the year."
—Hugh Grant

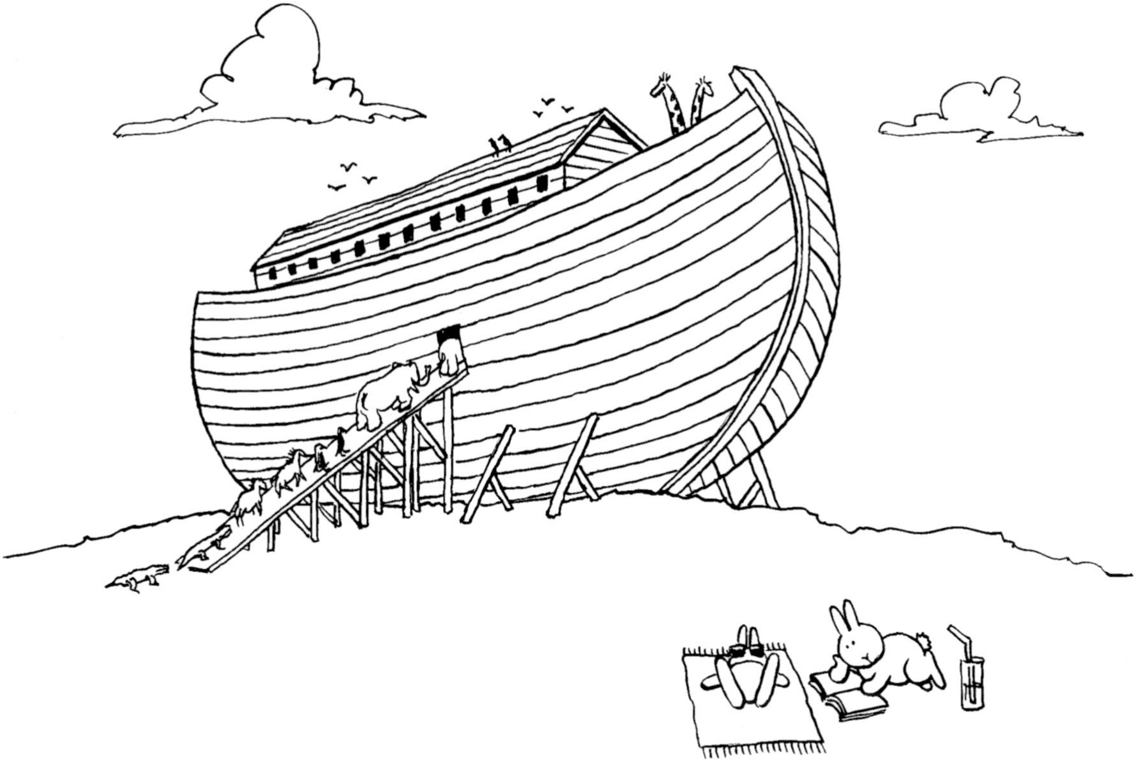

From: THE BOOK OF BUNNY SUICIDES

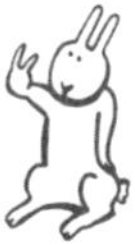

Little Fluffy Rabbits who Just Don't want to Live anymore

"It's the funniest, bunniest book I've ever read!"
—Elton John

"Brilliantly researched—one of the most important books of the year."
—Hugh Grant

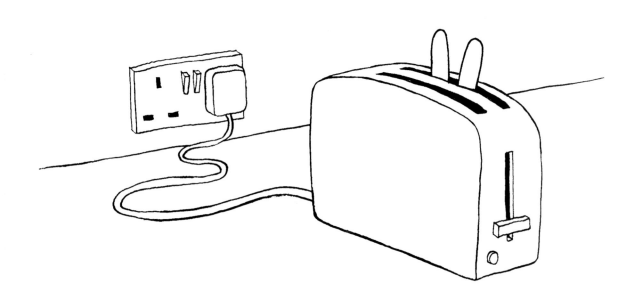

From: THE BOOK OF BUNNY SUICIDES

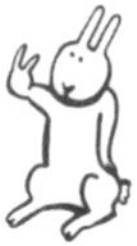

Little Fluffy Rabbits who Just Don't want to Live anymore

"It's the funniest, bunniest book I've ever read!"
—Elton John

"Brilliantly researched—one of the most important books of the year."
—Hugh Grant

From: THE BOOK OF BUNNY SUICIDES

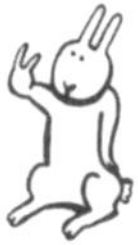

Little Fluffy Rabbits who Just Don't want to Live anymore

"It's the funniest, bunniest book I've ever read!"
—Elton John

"Brilliantly researched—one of the most important books of the year."
—Hugh Grant

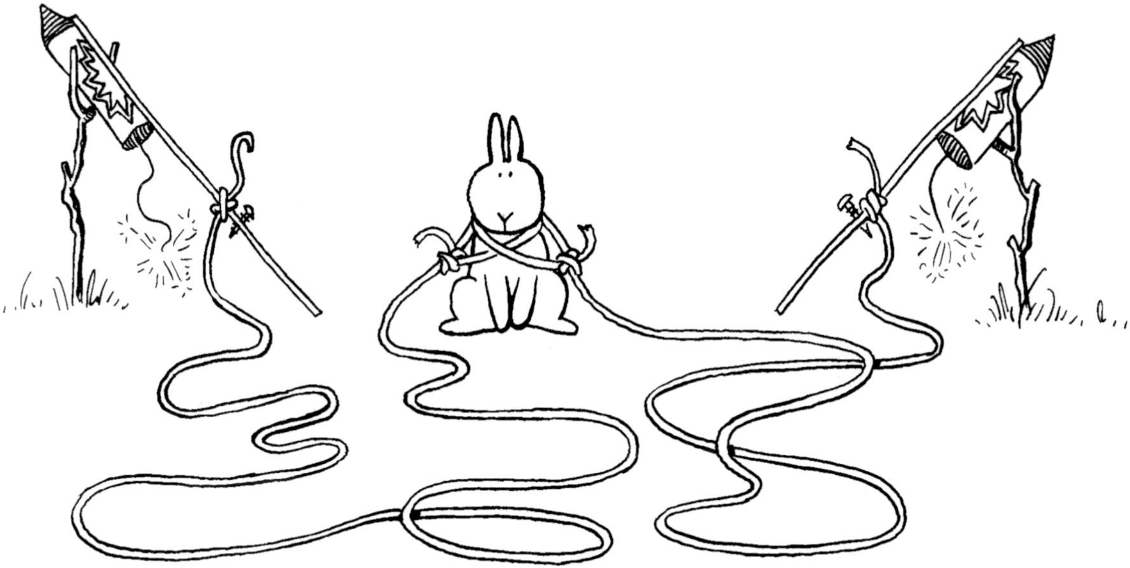

From: THE BOOK OF BUNNY SUICIDES

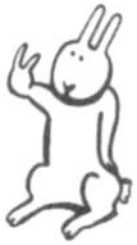

Little Fluffy Rabbits who Just Don't want to Live anymore

"It's the funniest, bunniest book I've ever read!"
—Elton John

"Brilliantly researched—one of the most important books of the year."
—Hugh Grant

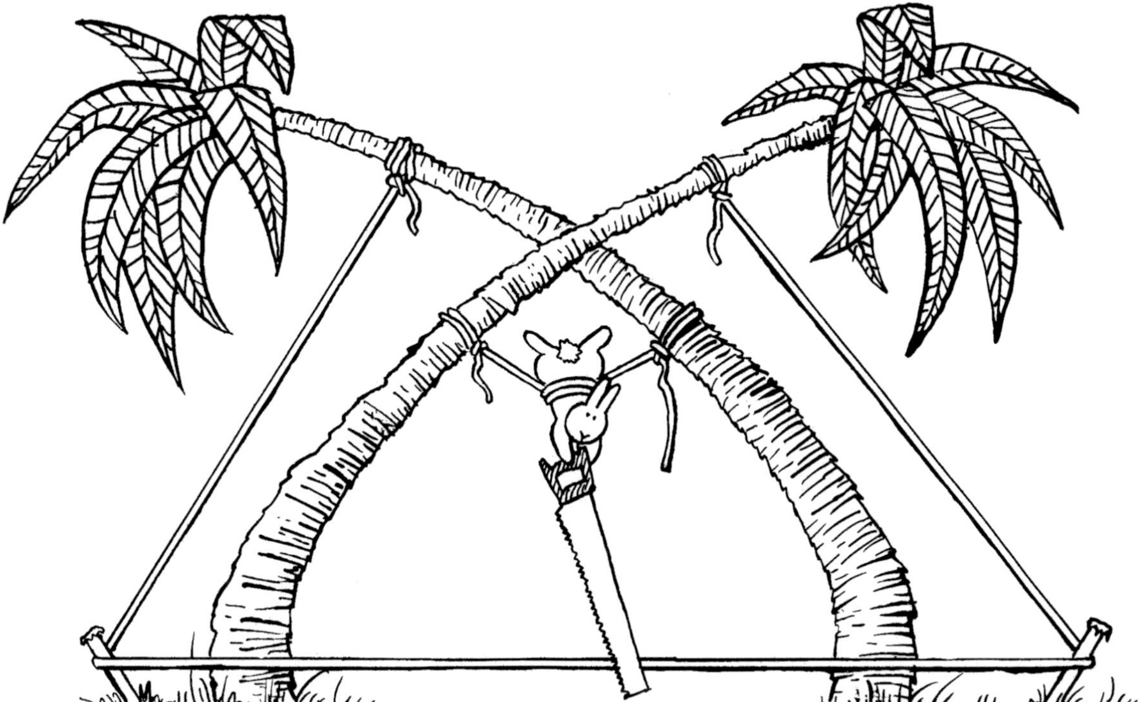

From: THE BOOK OF BUNNY SUICIDES

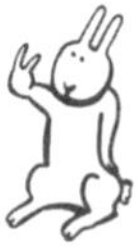

Little Fluffy Rabbits who Just Don't want to Live anymore

"It's the funniest, bunniest book I've ever read!"
—Elton John

"Brilliantly researched—one of the most important books of the year."
—Hugh Grant

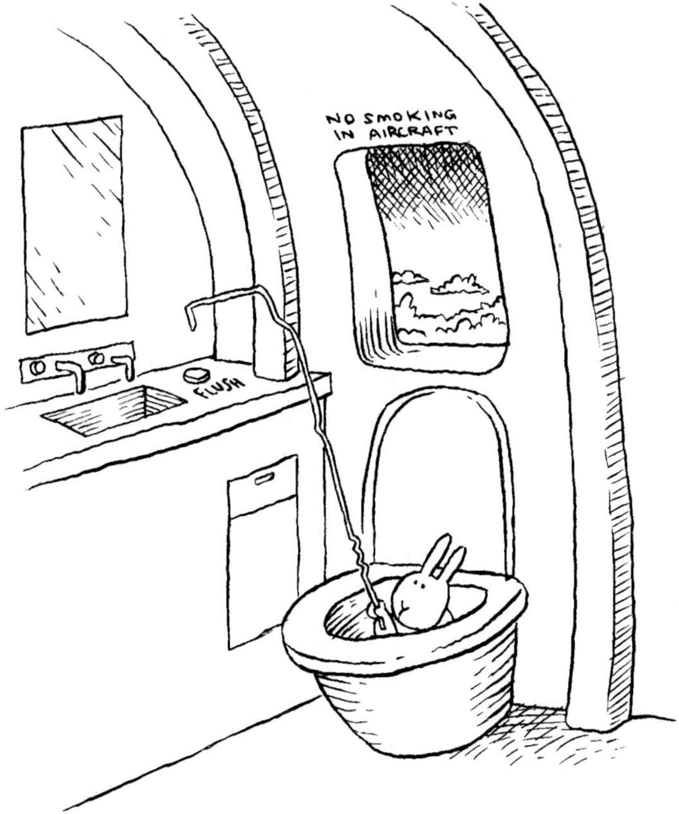
NO SMOKING IN AIRCRAFT
FLUSH

From: THE BOOK OF BUNNY SUICIDES

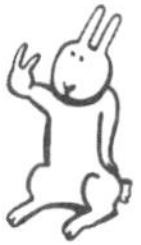

Little Fluffy Rabbits Who Just Don't Want to Live Anymore

"It's the funniest, bunniest book I've ever read!"
—Elton John

"Brilliantly researched—one of the most important books of the year."
—Hugh Grant

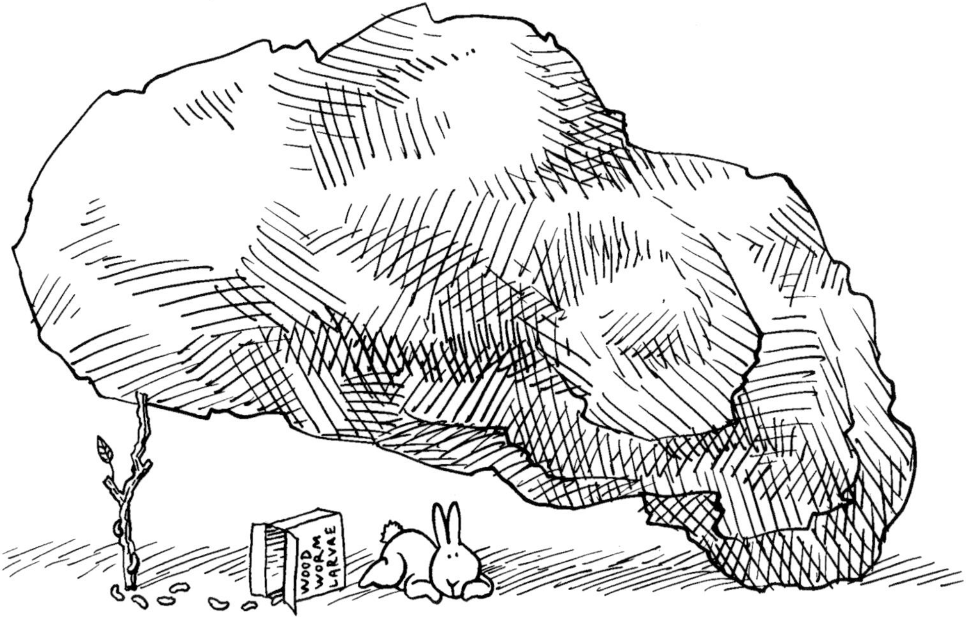
WOOD
WORM
LARVAE

From: THE BOOK OF BUNNY SUICIDES

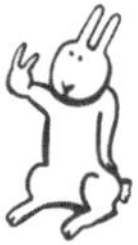

Little Fluffy Rabbits who Just Don't want to Live anymore

"It's the funniest, bunniest book I've ever read!"
—Elton John

"Brilliantly researched—one of the most important books of the year."
—Hugh Grant

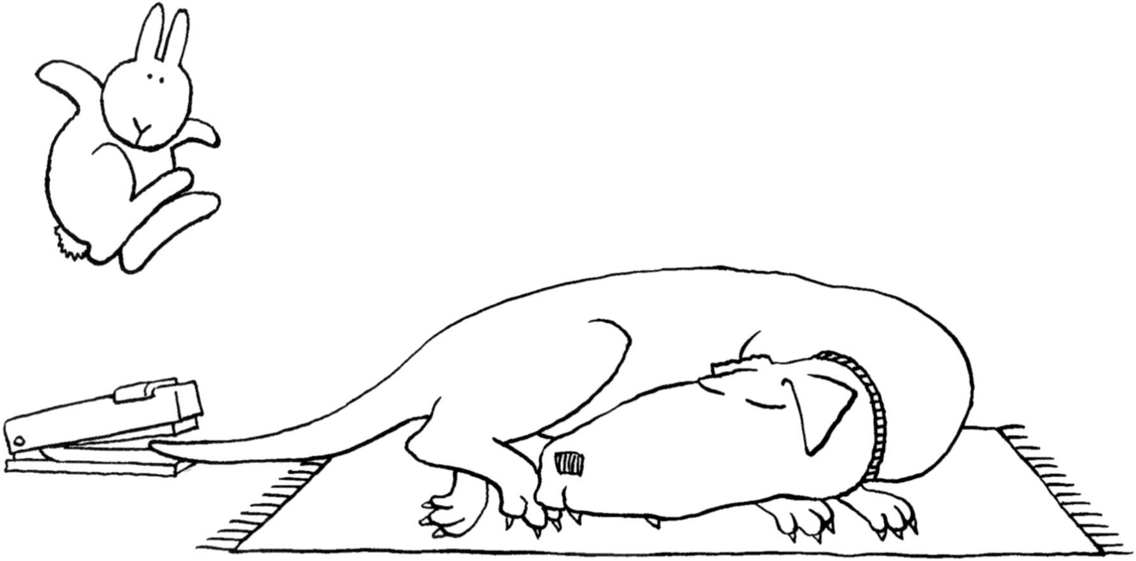

From: THE BOOK OF BUNNY SUICIDES

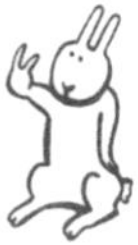

Little Fluffy Rabbits who Just Don't want to Live anymore

"It's the funniest, bunniest book I've ever read!"
—Elton John

"Brilliantly researched—one of the most important books of the year."
—Hugh Grant

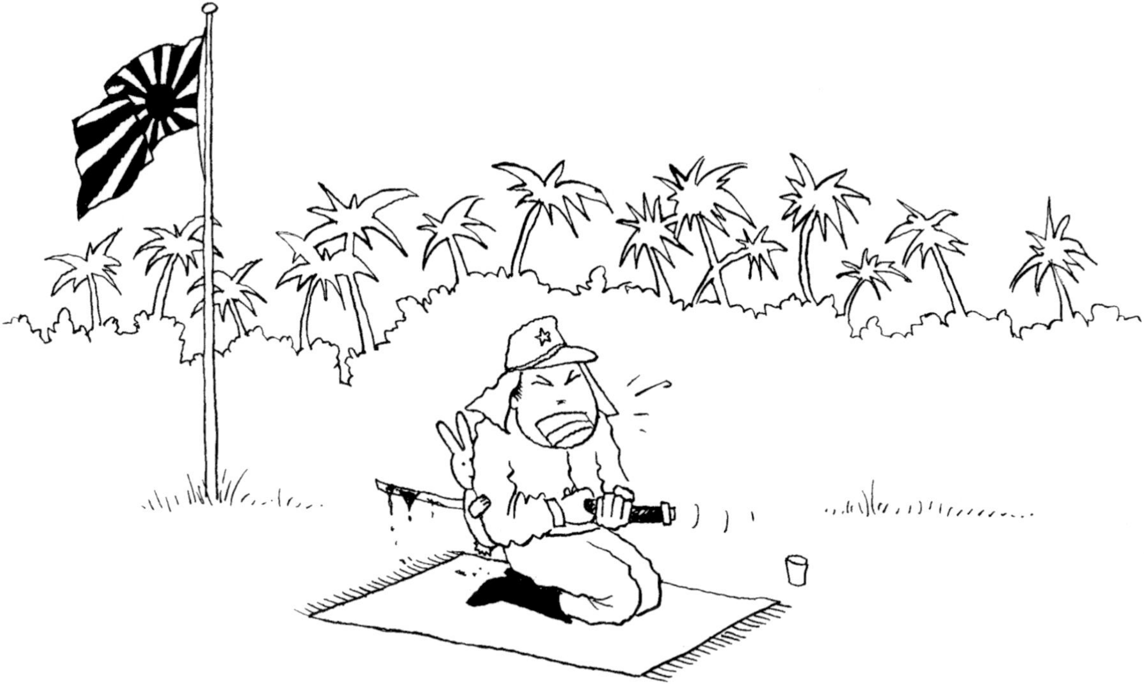

From: THE BOOK OF BUNNY SUICIDES

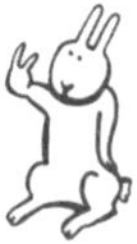

Little Fluffy Rabbits who Just Don't want to Live anymore

"It's the funniest, bunniest book I've ever read!"
—Elton John

"Brilliantly researched—one of the most important books of the year."
—Hugh Grant

From: THE BOOK OF BUNNY SUICIDES

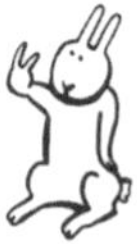

Little Fluffy Rabbits who Just Don't want to Live anymore

"It's the funniest, bunniest book I've ever read!"
—Elton John

"Brilliantly researched—one of the most important books of the year."
—Hugh Grant

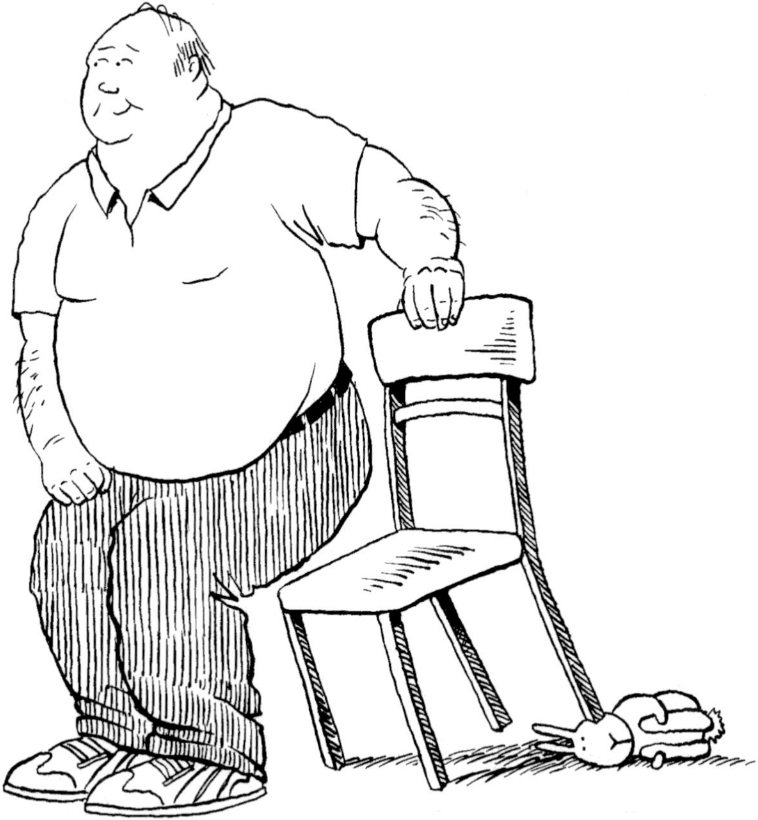

From: THE BOOK OF BUNNY SUICIDES 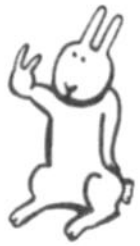

Little Fluffy Rabbits who Just Don't want to Live anymore

"It's the funniest, bunniest book I've ever read!"
—Elton John

"Brilliantly researched—one of the most important books of the year."
—Hugh Grant

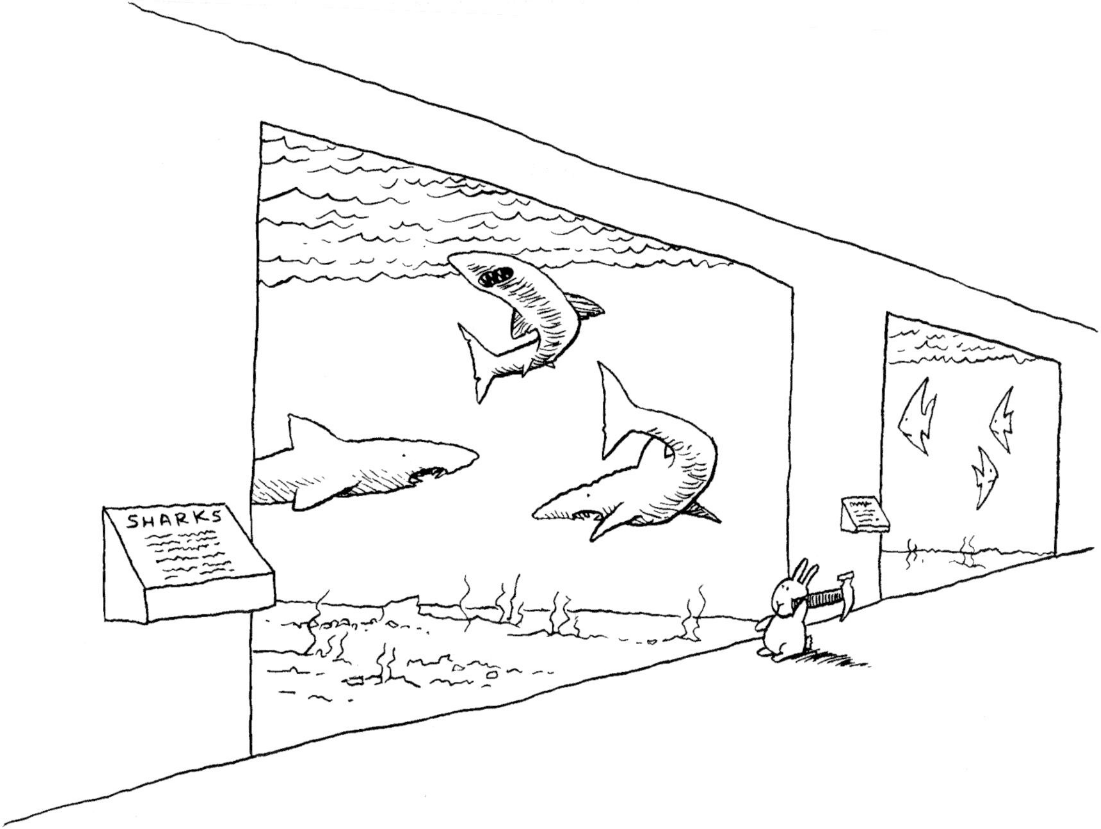
SHARKS

From: THE BOOK OF BUNNY SUICIDES

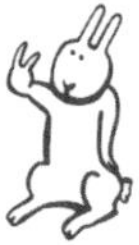

Little Fluffy Rabbits who Just Don't want to Live anymore

"It's the funniest, bunniest book I've ever read!"
—Elton John

"Brilliantly researched—one of the most important books of the year."
—Hugh Grant